PALEO BREAD

Gluten-Free Bread Recipes for a Paleo Diet

John Chatham

CONTENTS

INTRODUCTION

If you're one of the millions of people who suffer from such conditions as celiac disease, type 2 diabetes, heart disease, obesity, or digestive disorders, then you may be looking for a diet that can help you take control of your condition. Because all of these illnesses are affected by poor dietary choices, you may be considering the Paleo diet but have some reservations because of the restrictions. If so, read on!

Regardless of what literature you've read on the subject, most medical professionals agree that ingredients such as processed flours, white sugar, artificial preservatives, and empty calories are bad for you. Once you cut these unhealthful ingredients out of your diet, you're going to feel better, look better, and be healthier in general. The problem is that it sounds a whole lot easier than it actually is, at least in the beginning.

The Western diet is based almost entirely upon ingredients that make you sick. If you're like the typical American, you have a bagel made from processed flour and loaded with fattening cream cheese for breakfast, then you have a fast-food cheeseburger and fries for lunch, and perhaps spaghetti and meatballs with garlic bread for dinner. Oh, and don't forget the chips or cookies that you grab for a quick snack between meals and the ice cream that you have for dessert.

With all of that delicious convenience, it's no wonder that, as a country, we're literally eating ourselves to death!

For years, faithful followers of the Paleo diet and other diets that restrict all of those empty carbs and processed grains have sacrificed such foods as breads in order to reap the benefits of healthful eating. If you're one of those people who, by medical necessity or sheer willpower, have grudgingly chosen to give up bread solely because processed flour is horrible for you, then we've got great news: Bread is back, and it's delicious!

1

WHAT IS THE PALEO DIET?

Whether modern health care professionals want to admit it or not, the Paleo diet closely mirrors what most of them tell their patients: eat more fruits, vegetables, and lean meats, and stay away from processed garbage. The diet, also known as the Stone Age diet, the caveman diet, and the hunter-gatherer diet, has gained a significant following in recent years, and there's some pretty good research to support the switch.

How Did the Paleo Diet Start?

Back in the 1970s a gastroenterologist by the name of Walter L. Voegtlin observed that digestive diseases such as colitis, Crohn's disease, and irritable bowel syndrome were much more prevalent in people who followed a modern Western diet than it was in our ancestors, whose diet consisted largely of vegetables, fruits, nuts, and lean meats. He began treating patients with these disorders by recommending diets low in carbohydrates and high in animal fats.

Unfortunately, the medical world simply wasn't ready to give up the idea that a low-fat, low-calorie diet was the healthiest way to eat, so

Dr. Voegtlin's observations and research went largely unnoticed, and the Paleo diet was shoved to the back of the drawer.

Finally—The Stone Age Is Cool Again!

Fast forward a decade to a point when medical researchers had gained considerably more insight into how the human body actually works. Melvin Konner, S. Boyd Eaton, and Marjorie Shostak of Emory University published a book called *The Paleolithic Prescription: A Program of Diet and Exercise and a Design for Living*, then followed it up with a second book, *The Stone-Age Health Programme: Diet and Exercise as Nature Intended*. The first book became the foundation for most of the modern versions of the Paleo diet and the second backed it up with more research.

The main difference was that instead of eliminating any foods that our ancestors wouldn't have had access to as Dr. Voegtlin did originally, Konner, Eaton, and Shostak encouraged eating foods that were nutritionally and proportionally similar to a traditional caveman diet. Because it was more realistic, the diet caught on like wildfire, and the research in favor of it continues to grow.

What Are the Rules?

Paleo is one of the easiest diets on the planet to follow: just remember to keep it real. If it's processed, artificial, or otherwise not directly from the earth, don't eat it. It's that simple. Dairy is one of the foods that people debate allowing, and we'll discuss it later, but for now, it's forbidden. Here's a list of the delicious, healthful foods that the Paleo diet encourages:

- Eggs
- Healthful oils—olive and coconut are best; canola oil is under debate right now, too
- Lean animal proteins
- Nuts and seeds (note, however, that peanuts are *not* nuts)
- Organic fruits
- Organic vegetables
- Seafood, especially cold-water fish such as salmon and tuna in order to get the most omega-3 fatty acids

Sounds kind of familiar, doesn't it? That's because it's probably what your doctor encouraged you to eat more of the last time you went to see him or her! Now let's take a look at some foods that are off the table if you're going to eat Stone Age style:

- Alcohol
- Artificial foods, such as preservatives and zero-calorie sweeteners
- Cereal grains, such as wheat, barley, hops, corn, oats, rye, and rice
- Dairy (though some followers allow dairy for the health benefits)
- Legumes (including peanuts)
- Processed foods, such as wheat flour and sugar
- Processed meats, such as bacon, deli meats, sausage, and canned meats
- Starchy vegetables (though these are currently under debate)

Frequently Asked Questions

Now that you have a general idea of what you can and can't eat, you may still have a few questions, so we've put together a list of those most frequently asked.

Q. Why do you have to quit drinking?

A. Beer is basically liquid grain, and it's packed with empty calories. Many types of alcoholic products contain gluten, which we'll discuss in later chapters. Mixed drinks and wine are often loaded with sugar. If you absolutely can't go without that Friday-night cocktail, shoot for red wine, tequila, potato vodka, or white rum—and be careful what you mix it with.

Q. Why are legumes forbidden? They're natural foods and great sources of protein.

A. Most legumes, in their raw state, are toxic. They contain lectins— proteins that bind carbohydrates and have been shown to cause such autoimmune diseases as lupus and rheumatoid arthritis. The phytates in many legumes inhibit your absorption of critical minerals, and the protease inhibitors interfere with how your body breaks down protein.

Q. Why no dairy?

A. This one's under debate and there are many Paleo followers who still incorporate dairy regularly into their diets. The main reason that dairy is generally forbidden is that humans are the only animals who drink milk as adults, and many food allergies and digestive disorders are lactose-related. There's a much more scientific answer for this question, but it boils down to believing or not believing that milk is bad for you.

Q. How will I lose weight eating fat?

A. This is a question that most people have initially because we're all programmed to believe that red meat is bad for your heart. The fact is, lean, organic, free-range meat is an excellent source of protein and many other vitamins and minerals. You're not going to be living on it alone: you're going to be incorporating it into a healthful diet.

Q. Peanuts are nuts and corn is a vegetable, so why are they off-limits?

A. Au contraire. Peanuts are legumes and corn is a grain. Be careful that you know what food groups everything you eat falls into or you may sabotage your efforts to be healthier.

② THE BENEFITS OF PALEO

Many people turn to the Paleo diet because of the weight-loss benefits, but that's not where the idea originated. Of course, weight loss is a wonderful side effect that has its own set of healthful benefits.

When you add in the myriad other perks, going caveman is almost a no-brainer, especially now that you don't have to give up bread. Facing life without beans is one thing; giving up sandwiches is another! Let's take a quick peek at some of the biggest health benefits of following a Paleo diet.

Weight Loss

Since this is one of the primary reasons that many people decide to switch to a Paleo diet, we'll start here. Because you're eliminating empty carbs and adding in lots of healthful plant fiber and lean protein, losing weight will be much easier. A few other factors that contribute to healthful weight loss include:

- Plant fiber takes longer to digest, so you feel full longer.
- Lean proteins help keep your energy levels steady while you build muscle.

- Omega-3s help boost your metabolism and reduce body fat.
- You'll be eating a greater volume of food but taking in fewer calories.

The bottom line is that you'll be consuming foods that help your body function the way it's supposed to, and one of the natural side effects of that is weight loss.

Healthy Digestive System

The theory is that our bodies aren't adapted to eating grains, dairy, and other foods that are forbidden by the Paleo diet, and so they cause digestive upset, inflammation, and discomfort. Also, your digestive tract needs fiber to help it sweep food through your system or else it builds up and causes problems. Just some of the conditions that may be improved by going caveman include:

- Colitis
- Constipation
- Gas
- Heartburn
- Irritable bowel syndrome

Many people who begin the Paleo diet for other reasons, such as weight loss or heart health, report improved digestive health. Yet another reason that this incredible diet is worth your time!

Type 2 Diabetes Prevention

In the United States and other cultures that have adopted a Western diet, type 2 diabetes has reached disastrous proportions. Historically an adult disease, children are developing this debilitating illness at an alarming rate, and there's no sign of this trend changing. One of the main culprits is excess consumption of processed sugars and flours.

By simply eliminating these calorie-laden, nutritionless foods from your diet, you can literally save your own life. The Paleo diet helps you avoid type 2 diabetes as well as metabolic syndrome, a precursor to many different diseases, for the following reasons:

- Omega-3s help reduce belly fat, an indicator of diabetes and metabolic syndrome.
- Lean proteins and plant fiber help increase insulin resistance so that your sugar levels don't spike.
- The vitamin C that's so readily available in citrus fruits and colorful veggies helps reduce belly fat.
- Lean protein takes longer to metabolize so you avoid energy highs and lows.

Immune Health

When you eat foods that your body isn't adapted to, such as processed wheats, legumes, and dairy products, your body produces an allergic response in the form of inflammation, even if you don't experience any obvious outward symptoms. You may notice dark circles under your eyes as well as a feeling of general lethargy. You may attribute these symptoms to stress or exhaustion, but they're actually signs of a chronic allergy.

Inflammation in your body is a bad thing if it's occurring chronically, and it has been causally linked to such autoimmune disorders as:

- Fibromyalgia
- Lupus
- Multiple sclerosis
- Rheumatoid arthritis
- Several different types of cancer

The sad part here is that you don't even realize what you're doing to your body because there are often no symptoms until you have developed the disease. Switching to the Paleo diet may help reduce or eliminate your risk of many debilitating illnesses.

Cardiovascular Health

For most of your life, you've probably been told how horrible red meat and other animal proteins are for your heart, but recent research indicates that this is simply not true. Remember that there's a huge difference in scarfing down a fatty hamburger or sausage and enjoying a lean, organic, grass-fed steak. The burger and sausage are full of saturated fats and, most likely, hormones and additives.

On the other hand, steak is a lean, nutritious protein that delivers essential vitamins and minerals with very little bad fat and no empty calories, preservatives, or hormones. When you throw omega-3s and LDL-lowering healthful fats into the mix, you've got a heart-healthful meal that's good for anybody.

A Few Final Words on Health

The health benefits of giving up processed flour, refined sugar, and foods that cause inflammatory responses could fill an entire doctoral thesis, and the advantages to eliminating hormones and artificial additives from foods could fill another one. We didn't even touch on how a Paleo diet can help with allergies, cancer, brain health, joint health, or celiac disease, but we'll cover some of these as we discuss the health risks of gluten in the next chapter. Suffice it to say that the benefits of going Paleo far outweigh the relatively minor inconvenience of giving up a few foods.

3

THE TROUBLE WITH GLUTEN

We've discussed many of the health benefits of switching to a Paleo diet, but one of the main benefits is that foods allowed on the diet don't have gluten in them. For millions of people worldwide, eating caveman-style is a relatively simple way to avoid digestive upset and even cancers that are caused by an allergy to gluten.

What Is Gluten?

Latin for "glue," gluten is a protein found in wheats and grains that gives the ground flours elasticity and helps them to rise. It's also the binding component that gives bread its chewy texture and keeps it from crumbling apart after baking. Because gluten is insoluble in water, it can be removed from flour, but typically when you do that, you lose all of the good properties that make breads and cakes what they are.

Without gluten, your baked goods won't rise and they'll have a grainy, crumbly texture. They won't taste anything like their gluten-laden cousins, and you probably won't want to eat more than the first bite. Because of an increasing demand for gluten-free products, food corporations have dedicated a tremendous amount of time and money into creating tasty, effective gluten-free products. Unfortunately, most commercially prepared gluten-free recipe mixes still fall short.

Is the Paleo Diet Gluten-Free?

Because gluten naturally occurs in wheats and grains, the Paleo diet is completely gluten-free. All grain products are strictly forbidden. Remember, the original creator of the diet was a gastroenterologist developing a plan that would help his patients with gastric disorders. Gluten intolerance is one of the most prevalent causes of gastrointestinal distress in Western civilization.

What Is Gluten Intolerance?

Gluten intolerance, or celiac disease in its advanced stage, is a condition that damages the small intestine, and it's triggered by eating foods that have gluten in them. Some of these foods include:

- Bread
- Cookies
- Just about any baked good
- Most flours, including white and wheat flours
- Pasta
- Pizza dough

Gluten triggers an immune response in the small intestine that causes damage to its inside. This can lead to an inability to absorb vital nutrients. Other illnesses associated with this disease include lactose intolerance, bone loss, several types of cancer, neurological complications, and malnutrition. Diseases notwithstanding, just the symptoms of gluten intolerance can disrupt daily life. They include:

- Depression
- Fatigue
- Joint pain
- Neuropathy

- Osteoporosis
- Rashes
- Severe diarrhea
- Stomach cramps

These are only a few of the symptoms that a person with gluten intolerance can suffer from, and since all foods that contain gluten are forbidden on the Paleo diet, you can see what the appeal is.

The Harmful Effects of Gluten

Gluten doesn't just harm people with fully developed celiac disease. It's actually harmful to us all. Long-term studies indicate that people who have even a mild sensitivity to gluten exhibit a significantly higher risk of death than people who do not. The worst part is that 99 percent of people with gluten sensitivity don't even know they have it. They attribute their symptoms to other conditions, such as stress or fatigue.

Absorption Malfunction

One of the attributes that many obese or overweight people share is the fact that they can still feel hungry after eating a full meal. This feeling of hunger is because gluten sensitivity is preventing your body from absorbing vital nutrients.

Food Addiction

There are chemicals called exorphins in some foods that cause you to crave food even when you're not hungry. Food addiction is a serious issue and doesn't necessarily denote a lack of willpower; these exorphins are actually a drug-like chemical released in your brain that creates an irresistible desire for more food. Gluten contains as many as fifteen different exorphins.

Though food companies have created gluten-free foods, they often replace the gluten with flavor enhancers such as sodium and sugar, which can still seriously sabotage your dieting and fitness efforts. Another advantage to the Paleo diet is that by following it, you're not only eliminating gluten, you're also avoiding the pitfalls of commercially prepared foods that continue to make you sick.

Other Conditions Related to Gluten

There are numerous other conditions related to gluten sensitivity, and many professionals postulate that this is simply because our bodies aren't adapted to eating, grains so your body treats them as allergens. Other symptoms or disorders linked to eating gluten include:

- Anxiety
- Autism
- Dementia
- Migraines
- Mouth sores
- Schizophrenia
- Seizures

These aren't just minor aches and pains, though gluten sensitivity can cause those, too. These are major diseases and conditions that can ruin your life. It's no wonder that people who know they suffer from gluten intolerance consider the Paleo diet.

Still, giving up such a delicious staple food as bread is difficult. The thought of never having another sandwich is nearly enough to send a person running, but fortunately there are now some really great gluten-free bread recipes, such as the ones in Chapter 5, that will make it seem like you're giving up nothing!

Health Benefits of Going Gluten-Free

Obviously, there are countless benefits of giving up gluten, but here are a few that may be of particular interest to you:

- Decreased chance of several types of cancer
- Healthy, painless digestion
- Healthy skin
- Improved brain function
- Improved mood
- Reduced appetite
- Weight loss (or gain, if you're underweight because of malnutrition)

With the obvious advantages of giving up grains, it's difficult to understand exactly why people would hesitate. It's just a matter of making some adjustments to your diet, and now that understanding about both food and health is increasing, there are some great alternatives out there that will help you get rid of your addiction to grains!

4

PALEO FOOD GUIDE

S hopping for foods that are Paleo friendly can be a daunting task when you're first starting out. What's allowed and what's not? What are all of those mystery ingredients that are listed in foods? For the most part, stocking your fridge and pantry is fairly simple, but there are going to be times when you don't want to eat just steak and broccoli, and there will be other times when you need something fast and simple. Don't worry: you'll get the hang of it.

There are a few different versions of the Paleo diet, but for the sake of this discussion, we're going to take the modern middle road so that it's easier for you to make the transition to your new, healthier lifestyle. Throughout the following paragraphs, we're going to discuss what foods are OK and where you can find them. We'll also discuss some alternate ingredients for baking bread and other goodies that won't get you kicked out of the cave!

Paleo Pantry and Kitchen Tips

The first bit of good news is that you're not going to be counting calories. Instead, you're going to try to keep your portions in line with what your ancestors most likely ate. A diet that consists of 50 to 60 percent protein,

30 to 40 percent healthful carbs, and 5 to 10 percent healthful vegetable fats such as olive oil, avocados, nuts, and seeds is the general goal.

Basically, when you're stacking your plate, put your protein on one side and your fruits and veggies on the other. Be careful with nuts and fruits; though they're good for you, they're high in calories and can sabotage your weight-loss efforts if you're not careful.

If Possible, Go Raw

Many fruits and vegetables lose nutritional value when you cook them, so when possible, eat them raw. You'll also eat less because you'll be chewing more. If you opt to cook your veggies, steam them lightly so that they maintain their bright colors. A key clue that you've cooked your greens to death is that they've lost that pretty vibrant green hue and turned an olive color. Try to avoid that.

Steaming, baking, grilling, and broiling are all great methods of cooking and require little added fat to prevent sticking. It should go without saying that the fryer can go in the garage to be sold at your next rummage sale.

Cooking on the Fly

Meals away from home can be a real challenge when you're first start-ing out. Restaurants are filled with tempting burgers and fries, and you have no idea what's in the salad dressings. If you must eat out, order a plain garden salad with oil and vinegar. You could also request a steak or chicken breast to go on top but make sure that they either grill it dry or use olive oil.

Opt not to eat out in the beginning. Instead, make an amazing soup at home for dinner with enough leftover that you aren't tempted to go out for a quick fix. That way, you know what's in your food and you know that it's going to be delicious!

Plan Ahead

If you know in advance what you're going to eat for lunch or for dinner, you're not going to be as likely to cheat with something quick from the vending machine. Take snacks to work with you so that the box of doughnuts isn't so tempting. Here's a food list to help you get your pantry stocked up and ready to rock Stone Age style.

Meats and Proteins

Your meats need to come from grass-fed, organic livestock, free-range poultry, or wild-caught fish and seafood. Wild game is great, too, if you're so inclined. Actually, meats such as venison are extremely low in bad fats and high in good fats and lean protein, so feel free to partake!

Fruits and Vegetables

If at all possible, shop at your local farmers' market for fresh organic fruits and veggies. Since the Paleo diet is dependent upon your creativity to complete a hot, fresh, delicious meal without the aid of flours, fats, and no-no's, you're going to have to learn a number of ways to prepare dishes. Plus, if you're offering a wide variety of foods that your family knows and loves, you won't be under so much pressure to create a single main dish that everybody will eat and enjoy.

Tomatoes are a great addition to any salad and make a flavorful base for soups and sauces. They're packed with nutrients and have so many uses that you should always have some on hand. Other staples should include carrots, peppers, cauliflower, and celery.

For fruits, opt for ones that are high in nutrients and relatively low in sugar, such as stone fruits and berries. Berries are also fabulous sources of antioxidants, phytonutrients, and vitamins. Apples are an easy grab-and-go food, as are peaches, oranges, and bananas. The dark tip of the banana that you usually pick off is rich in vitamin K, so eat it!

Oils and Fats

Oils high in saturated fats, such as corn oil and vegetable oil, are out. Opt instead for oils that are high in omega-3s such as olive oil, avocado oil, coconut oil, and possibly canola oil. The latter is currently a point of contention among long-term Paleo followers, but there's a compelling argument to include it.

Seasonings

Your success with making the transition to the caveman way of eating is largely dependent on how flavorful your food is. As a result, you're going to need to incorporate various herbs and spices in order to make your dishes delicious. Here are a few that you should always have on hand:

- Allspice
- Black pepper
- Basil
- Cayenne pepper
- Cinnamon
- Cloves
- Crushed red pepper
- Curry powder
- Dry mustard
- Garlic—fresh and powdered
- Mustard seed
- Oregano
- Paprika
- Parsley
- Rosemary
- Thyme

Finally, you'll probably want to keep some snacks on hand. Now, that does *not* mean cupcakes, potato chips, or crackers. However, there are still many options, such as certain beef jerkies (or even better, make your own!), dried fruits, nuts, and seeds. They're satisfying and add nutrients to your diet instead of unhealthful fats.

Paleo Shopping Tips

Going to the grocery store is going to be a bit of a challenge at first, just as it is anytime you make changes to your diet. Especially if you're accustomed to eating a large amount of refined flour and sugar and aren't yet over your sugar addiction, it's not going to be easy. It's OK though—we have a few tips to help you along your way.

- Shop for your produce at the local farmers' market if possible.
- When at the grocery store, shop around the perimeter of the store. That's where most stores keep all of their meats and produce, and 99 percent of your food is going to come from those departments. If you need to get something from an aisle, go straight in, get it, and get back to the perimeter before those cookies catch your eye!
- Make a list and stick to it.
- If you do choose to eat canned fruits and veggies, make sure that you read the label so that you're not getting hidden sodium and preservatives.
- Buy meat in bulk when you catch a sale.
- Don't shop hungry! Have a low-fat, high-protein snack before you go so that you aren't tempted while you're there.

Alternative Ingredients for Baking Paleo

So if you can't use flour, animal milk, or sugar, does that mean that you'll never have another sandwich or muffin? Absolutely not. Due to the massive increase in demand for gluten-free baking products, there are now several different Paleo-friendly options available to give you something to toast with your fruit in the morning. The great thing is that, unlike first-generation gluten-free flours, the latest creations are not only healthful, but delicious, too.

- **Almond flour/meal:** Almond flour is made from finely ground blanched almonds. Almond meal is simply unblanched almonds ground up with their skins on, and it is much coarser. Flour is generally the best option for baking if you're looking for a substitute. It lends a mildly nutty flavor to your recipes.
- **Coconut flour:** This flour is made from coconut meat after the milk is extracted. It's extremely high in fiber and low in digestible carbs. Because it's so high in fiber, it's great as a weight-loss aid; studies have actually shown that consuming a product with 1/4 cup coconut flour can decrease caloric intake by as much as 10 percent.
- **Golden flaxseed:** This is a bit coarser than almond or coconut flours, so the bread texture will be significantly different unless you mix it with finer-ground flours. It lends a nutty flavor to your baked goods. The health benefits of flax are numerous: it acts as an anti-inflammatory, helps prevent heart disease, and lowers your blood pressure and cholesterol. Flax is also a fabulous source of fiber.
- **Coconut oil:** There are a wide range of health benefits derived from coconut oil. It's good for your heart, your digestion, your immune system, and is also useful in helping with weight loss. It has a light but distinct coconut flavor.

- **Almond butter:** Almonds are high on nearly every single "world's healthiest foods" list on the planet because they're amazing for you. Almond butter gives a nice nutty flavor reminiscent of peanut butter to your dishes.
- **Cashew butter:** Rich in several different vitamins, cashew butter is also high in protein and is a good substitute for butter or peanut butter in a recipe. It does, of course, taste like cashews.
- **Macadamia butter:** Macadamia nuts are a rich source of dietary fiber and monounsaturated fats. The butter is sweet and creamy and helps reduce bad cholesterol while increasing good cholesterol. Macadamia butter is a good replacement for regular butter and has a sweet, nutty flavor.
- **Almond milk:** Pressed from the flesh of almonds, almond milk is high in protein and low in bad fats. It's a healthful, delicious replacement for dairy and has an extremely mild nutty flavor that is barely noticeable.
- **Coconut milk:** Pressed from the meat of the coconut, coconut milk helps maintain stable blood sugar and promotes cardiovascular, bone, muscle, and nerve health. It gives a rich, sweet coconut flavor to your dishes.

All of these alternative ingredients add luscious flavors to your dishes and will really make them more multidimensional than traditional white flour and animal milk would. You're also getting multiple nutritional benefits that you wouldn't get with old-school ingredients, so give them a try! By the way, honey is a Paleo-friendly ingredient that can be used sparingly as a sweetener in baked goods.

Now that you have a decent grasp of why you should transition to the Paleo way of living and how you can get started, we'll give you some final tips for being successful on your new journey, then we'll get into the Paleo bread recipes!

10 Tips for Living Paleo

Just as with any change, adjusting to the Paleo diet will take you some time. After all, you're not only changing your diet, you're also changing the way you think about food. Ingredients that you've known and loved for most of your life are now strictly off-limits. If you're allowing yourself to have caffeine (which many Paleo dieters do not), then it's probably the only part of your morning meal that will remain the same.

Now you're going to be eating plenty of fruits, vegetables, and lean proteins, so you shouldn't ever be hungry. If you are, just eat something! You're not going to be counting calories but you still need to be cautious about what you eat because, just like in most diets, all Paleo-approved foods are *not* equal. You're going to hit some rough spots, too, so here are some tips to get you through.

1. Go Cold Turkey

If you're serious about changing your lifestyle and want to be successful with your transition, submerge yourself in it completely. Clear all of the non-Paleo foods from your pantry and your fridge and head to the grocery store. Don't buy anything that isn't on your list, and don't stop for a "final burger" on your way home.

2. Stick with It

For the first week or so, you'll probably have decreased energy because you're not eating a ton of sugar and empty carbs. Your body will have to adapt to burning proteins and complex carbs for energy. Just push through it and remember that if you do, you're going to have more energy than ever once your sugar addiction is over.

3. Think Positive

This is a positive life change, not a trip to the gallows. Don't look for ways to cheat or try to find loopholes, because the only person you're cheating is yourself. If you find that the diet is too difficult to follow, or if your energy levels are flagging, feed a few more carbs back into your diet and allow your body to adjust slowly.

4. Head to the Gym

There's nothing that makes you feel more of a sense of accomplishment than going to the gym and getting in a good workout. It has a way of making you want to eat healthful foods and take better care of yourself, so it's a great tool to help you stick with it.

5. Give It a Month

You're probably not going to be feeling so great for the first week on the diet, so that's not a good time to make a decision regarding your health. By week two, you're going to be through your detox and gaining steam, but you'll still be longingly eyeing the chips. Give the Paleo diet a chance for a full thirty days, and if you haven't gotten the results that you were looking for, then you may consider whether it's right for you, but don't give up too early.

6. Don't Fear the Fat

You've most likely been told for years that fat is bad. Avoid fat. Fat makes you fat. Fat makes you sick. Well, some fats do but not the healthful ones that you'll be eating on the Paleo diet, so go ahead and eat without fear. Trim extra fat off and cook using methods that allow for the most fat to cook off, but don't obsess about it; there are good fats and bad fats, and Paleo foods are generally the good kind.

7. Plan Ahead

This is probably one of the biggest keys to your success. Don't get stuck out in public with no food when hunger strikes because that will tempt you to head to those golden arches. Instead, prepare in advance so that you have healthful meals and snacks ready to eat when you need them.

8. Transition with a Friend

As with any other diet, you'll have a better rate of success if you start with a friend. It'll be even better if you start with a spouse or significant other, because they're right there under the same roof with you and can provide support.

9. Beware of Wolves in Sheep's Clothing

Many foods will claim to be Paleo friendly but won't be. They'll have some kind of artificial garbage, sugar, or gluten in them that will make them inedible. If nothing else, they may contain lots of calories or forbidden oils. Just be careful and read your labels.

10. Eat What You Like

Just because you're changing the way that you eat doesn't mean that you have to give up the foods that you love. Find ways to modify your favorite recipes so that you're still eating foods you enjoy. Speaking of which, let's move on to some really amazing bread recipes!

PALEO BREAD RECIPES

Paleo Banana Bread

The bananas in this moist and tender bread are what make it so delicious. The bread is easy to prepare and makes a healthful snack when you don't have time to sit down for a meal. Feel free to add the nuts of your choice for a little texture and more protein, but it's really delicious as is.

• 2 cups blanched almond flour	• 1/2 cup cold water
• 1 tablespoon ground cinnamon	• 1 teaspoon pure vanilla extract
• 1 teaspoon baking soda	• 1/4 cup raw honey
• 2 large eggs	• 2 overripe bananas, mashed

Preheat the oven to 350 degrees F. Lightly grease a standard loaf pan with cooking spray or coconut oil and set aside.

In a medium bowl, sift together the almond flour, cinnamon, and baking soda, and stir to combine well.

In a large bowl, using an electric mixer, beat the eggs until frothy. Add the water, vanilla, and honey, and beat until well combined. Stir in the mashed bananas and mix well.

Carefully add the flour mixture to the wet ingredients and stir until just combined. Pour the batter into the prepared pan and bake for 35 to 40 minutes, or until the top of the bread is browned and the edges are crisp. A toothpick inserted into the center should come out clean.

Allow the bread to cool completely before slicing and serving. Store any leftover slices in an airtight container or wrapped in plastic wrap for up to 3 days.

Makes 1 loaf (8 to 10 slices)

Coconut Bread

Shredded coconut paired with honey and vanilla make a deliciously scented, and even better-tasting, bread that will fit into your Paleo diet plan perfectly. Be sure to use unsweetened coconut flakes to avoid unnecessary sugar.

- 6 large eggs
- 2 teaspoons pure vanilla extract
- 2 tablespoons raw honey
- 3 cups unsweetened shredded coconut
- 1 teaspoon baking powder

Preheat the oven to 300 degrees F. Lightly grease a standard loaf pan with cooking spray or coconut oil and set aside.

In a large bowl, using an electric mixer, beat the eggs, vanilla, and honey until frothy and well combined.

Place the shredded coconut in a food processor and pulse until it becomes a fine flour, being careful not to overprocess it. Add the baking powder to the coconut flour and stir gently to combine.

Add the flour mixture to the wet ingredients and stir until just combined. Pour the batter into the prepared pan and bake for 35 to 40 minutes, or until a toothpick inserted into the center of the bread comes out clean.

Allow the bread to cool completely on a wire rack before removing it from the pan. Slice and serve with butter, nut butter, or Paleo-approved jam. Store any leftover slices in an airtight container or wrapped in plastic wrap for up to 3 days.

Makes 1 loaf (8 to 10 slices)

Almond Sweet Bread

This easy-to-prepare bread is perfect for morning toast, or just to enjoy as a sweet treat when you have a craving. Lightly toasted almonds add crunch, while raw honey adds a hint of sweetness that complements the almond flavoring well.

- 2 cups blanched almond flour
- 2 teaspoons baking powder
- 4 large eggs
- 1/2 cup coconut oil
- 1/4 cup raw honey
- 1 teaspoon almond extract
- 1/2 cup water
- 1/2 cup toasted almond slices

Preheat the oven to 350 degrees F. Lightly grease a standard loaf pan with cooking spray or coconut oil and set aside.

In a medium bowl, combine the almond flour and baking powder.

In a large bowl, using an electric mixer, beat the eggs with the coconut oil and honey. Add the almond extract and water, and stir well to combine.

Add the flour mixture to the wet ingredients and stir until just combined. Pour the batter into the prepared pan and sprinkle the almond slices over the top. Bake for 30 to 40 minutes, or until a toothpick inserted into the center of the bread comes out clean.

Allow the bread to cool completely on a wire rack before removing it from the pan. Slice and serve with butter or Paleo-approved jam. Store any leftover slices in an airtight container or wrapped in plastic wrap for up to 3 days.

Makes 1 loaf (8 to 10 slices)

Pumpkin Bread

Most of us think of pie when we hear the word pumpkin, *but this winter squash is actually a true health food in its own right. Loaded with fiber, vitamins, and minerals, it's a great addition to your Paleo diet. The best part is that buying canned pureed pumpkin is easy and inexpensive, making this delicious sweet bread a healthful treat that is super quick to put together. Be sure when buying canned pumpkin that you get pure pumpkin puree and not pie filling, which is loaded with sugar and seasonings.*

- 1 cup blanched almond flour
- 1 teaspoon baking soda
- 2 teaspoons ground cinnamon
- 1/4 teaspoon ground nutmeg
- 1/4 teaspoon ground cloves
- 1/2 cup pumpkin puree (canned or freshly roasted)
- 3 tablespoons raw honey
- 3 large eggs

Preheat the oven to 350 degrees F. Grease a standard loaf pan with cooking spray or coconut oil and set aside.

In a medium bowl, stir together the almond flour, baking soda, cinnamon, nutmeg, and cloves.

In a large bowl, using an electric mixer, beat the pumpkin puree, honey, and eggs until frothy.

Carefully add the flour mixture to the wet ingredients and stir until just combined. Pour the batter into the prepared pan and bake for 30 to 40 minutes, or until the top of the bread is lightly browned and a toothpick inserted into the center comes out clean.

Allow the bread to cool completely on a wire rack before removing it from the pan. Slice and serve. Store any leftover slices in an airtight container or wrapped in plastic wrap for up to 3 days.

Makes 1 loaf (8 to 10 slices)

Cherry Chocolate-Chip Bread

Pureed pumpkin and mashed banana give this bread a super moist, excellent texture that will make you crave this delicious bread. You'd never know it was gluten free and healthful after taking one bite, and we're betting it will become a regular in your Paleo recipe collection.

- 1 overripe banana, mashed
- 1/4 cup canned pumpkin puree
- 2 tablespoons safflower oil
- 2 large eggs
- 1 tablespoon raw honey
- 1 tablespoon pure vanilla extract
- 2 cups blanched almond flour
- 1 teaspoon baking soda
- 1 teaspoon baking powder
- 1/2 teaspoon ground cinnamon
- 1/2 cup unsweetened dried cherries
- 1/4 cup dark chocolate chips

Preheat the oven to 350 degrees F. Lightly grease a standard loaf pan with cooking spray or coconut oil and set aside.

In a large bowl, combine the mashed banana, pumpkin puree, and safflower oil. Add the eggs, one at a time, followed by the honey and vanilla, and stir well to combine.

In a medium bowl, combine the almond flour, baking soda, baking powder, and cinnamon.

Add the flour mixture to the wet ingredients and stir until well combined. Carefully fold in the cherries and chocolate chips.

Pour the batter into the prepared pan and bake for 35 to 40 minutes, or until the top of the bread is browned and a toothpick inserted into the center comes out clean.

Allow the bread to cool completely on a wire rack before removing it from the pan. Slice and serve. Store any leftover slices in an airtight container or wrapped in plastic wrap for up to 3 days.

Makes 1 loaf (8 to 10 slices)

Lemon Poppy Seed Bread

This tender bread is a gluten-free version of a popular quick bread, and it's just as easy to throw together. In fact, chances are you'll want to make it again and again. Looking for a variation? Try swapping orange zest for the lemon for a delicious alternate version of this classic.

- 2 cups blanched almond flour
- 2 teaspoons baking powder
- 4 large eggs
- 1/2 cup coconut oil
- 1/4 cup raw honey
- Zest of 1 lemon
- 1/2 cup water
- 2 tablespoons poppy seeds

Preheat the oven to 350 degrees F. Lightly grease a standard loaf pan with coconut oil or cooking spray and set aside.

In a medium bowl, stir together the flour and baking powder until combined.

In a large bowl, using an electric mixer, beat the eggs, coconut oil, and honey. Add the lemon zest and water, and stir to combine.

Add the flour mixture to the wet ingredients and stir until well combined. Fold in the poppy seeds. Pour the batter into the prepared pan and bake for 30 to 40 minutes, or until a toothpick inserted into the center of the bread comes out clean.

Allow the bread to cool completely on a wire rack before removing it from the pan. Slice and serve with butter, if desired. Store any leftover slices in an airtight container or wrapped in plastic wrap for up to 3 days.

Makes 1 loaf (8 to 10 slices)

Spiced Nut Bread

The smell of this bread baking will make you think of a cool fall day just before the holiday season begins; in fact, it's great for holiday parties or even as a healthful gift for someone following the Paleo diet plan. Full of flavor, this warm and spicy quick bread is a treat all year long.

- 2 cups blanched almond flour
- 1 teaspoon baking soda
- 1 tablespoon ground cinnamon
- 1 teaspoon ground ginger
- 1/2 teaspoon ground cloves
- 1/4 teaspoon ground nutmeg

- 2 large eggs
- 1/2 cup cold water
- 1 teaspoon pure vanilla extract
- 1/4 cup pure maple syrup
- 1/2 cup unsweetened applesauce

Preheat the oven to 350 degrees F. Lightly grease a standard loaf pan with cooking spray or coconut oil and set aside.

In a medium bowl, sift together the almond flour, baking soda, cinnamon, ginger, cloves, and nutmeg until well combined.

In a large bowl, using an electric mixer, beat the eggs until frothy. Add the water, vanilla, and maple syrup, and beat until well combined. Stir in the applesauce and mix well.

Carefully add the flour mixture to the wet ingredients and stir until just combined. Pour the batter into the prepared pan and bake for 35 to 40 minutes, or until the top of the bread is browned and the edges are crisp. A toothpick inserted into the center should come out clean.

Allow the bread to cool completely on a wire rack before removing it from the pan. Slice and serve. Store any leftover slices in an airtight container or wrapped in plastic wrap for up to 3 days.

Makes 1 loaf (8 to 10 slices)

Savory Breads

Paleo Pretzel Sticks

These are a healthful alternative to traditionally doughy and starchy pretzels and make a great addition to a big salad or Paleo stew. This basic recipe is easy to whip up and also easy to alter by adding herbs and spices to the dough that match your meal. You can make these savory breadsticks into a sweeter version by sprinkling them with cinnamon before baking, if you desire.

- 3 large eggs
- 2 cups blanched almond flour
- 1/4 cup coconut flour
- 2 tablespoons unsalted butter, melted
- 1 tablespoon water
- 1 egg white, beaten
- Coarse sea salt for topping (optional)

Preheat the oven to 350 degrees F. Line a large baking sheet with parchment paper and set aside.

In a medium bowl, using an electric mixer, beat the eggs until light yellow and frothy.

In a large bowl, stir together the almond and coconut flours and melted butter until well combined, then stir in the water.

Add the eggs to the flour mixture and stir until well combined. Allow the dough to rest for 5 minutes, then stir again, adding a little more water if necessary to make the dough pliable and easy to knead. The dough should be lightly sticky but not wet. Allow the dough to rest for 5 more minutes.

Divide the dough into 12 equal pieces. Roll each one into a breadstick, or shape into a pretzel if desired, and position on the parchment-lined pan.

Brush each breadstick with egg white. Top with sea salt if using, and bake for 10 to 15 minutes, or until the breadsticks are lightly browned.

Serve warm or at room temperature. Store any leftover breadsticks in an airtight container or wrapped in plastic wrap for up to 3 days.

Makes 1 dozen breadsticks

Rosemary Bread

This rustic bread is similar to focaccia, except that it is much better for you, as it fits in the Paleo diet. It comes together fairly easily and goes perfectly with soups and stews or alongside any meal.

- 1/4 cup blanched almond flour
- 1/4 cup arrowroot flour
- 1 teaspoon baking soda
- 3/4 cup natural raw almond butter
- 1 tablespoon raw honey

- 3 large eggs
- 2 tablespoons finely chopped rosemary
- 3 tablespoons olive oil
- Coarse sea salt for topping (optional)

Preheat the oven to 350 degrees F. Line a 9 x 13–inch jelly roll pan with parchment paper and set aside.

In a small bowl, stir together the almond and arrowroot flours and baking soda until combined.

In a large bowl, combine the almond butter and honey. Add the eggs, one at a time, stirring between each addition. Stir in the rosemary.

Add the flour mixture to the wet ingredients and stir until a wet dough forms.

Drizzle the olive oil on the parchment-lined pan and spread the dough over it. Allow the dough to rest for 5 minutes.

Bake for 25 to 30 minutes, or until the top of the bread is golden brown. Top with sea salt if desired. Allow the bread to cool.

Slice and serve alongside a meal or as a snack. Store any leftover bread in an airtight container or wrapped in plastic for up to 3 days.

Makes 12 servings

Sunflower Bread

Crunchy sunflower seeds make this savory, soft loaf of bread a hit when you're looking for something to complement soup or salad. They also provide plenty of heart-healthful fats, a little bit of protein, and some much-needed fiber into your diet. While there is a tiny bit of honey in this recipe, don't be fooled; it doesn't make this bread sweet.

- 1 cup blanched almond flour
- 1/2 cup ground golden flaxseed
- 1 teaspoon baking soda
- 1 teaspoon cream of tartar
- 3 large eggs
- 2 tablespoons olive oil
- 2 tablespoons water
- 1 teaspoon honey
- 1/2 cup shelled raw sunflower seeds, divided

Preheat the oven to 350 degrees F. Lightly grease a standard loaf pan with cooking spray or coconut oil and set aside.

In a medium bowl, stir together the flour, flaxseed, baking soda, and cream of tartar until well combined.

In a large bowl, using an electric mixer, beat the eggs until frothy, then stir in the olive oil, water, and honey. Add the flour mixture to the wet ingredients and stir until just combined. Fold in 1/4 cup of the sunflower seeds.

Pour the batter into the prepared pan, sprinkle with the remaining sunflower seeds, and bake for 25 to 30 minutes, or until the top of the bread is dark brown.

Allow the bread to cool completely on a wire rack before removing it from the pan. In order to preserve freshness, slice only what is being served. Store any leftover bread in an airtight container or wrapped in plastic wrap for up to 3 days.

Makes 1 loaf (8 to 10 slices)

Flaxseed Focaccia

Flaxseeds are an amazing superfood and perfect for Paleo bread, since when they are ground they have the texture of flour. This easy focaccia bread has a nutty taste, thanks in part to the flaxseed, but also due to the natural almond butter used to bind the dough. Serve this bread alongside a big green salad for a hearty meal that will leave you feeling full but not bloated.

- 1 cup ground golden flaxseed
- 1/4 cup blanched almond flour
- 1 teaspoon baking soda
- 3/4 cup natural raw almond butter
- 1 tablespoon raw honey
- 3 large eggs
- 3 tablespoons olive oil

Preheat the oven to 350 degrees F. Line a 9 x 13–inch jelly roll pan with parchment paper and set aside.

In a small bowl, stir together the flaxseed, almond flour, and baking soda until combined.

In a large bowl, combine the almond butter and honey. Add in the eggs, one at a time, stirring between each addition.

Add the flour mixture to the wet ingredients and stir until a wet dough forms.

Drizzle the olive oil on the parchment-lined pan and spread the dough over it. Allow the dough to rest for 5 minutes.

Bake for 25 to 30 minutes, or until the top of the focaccia is golden brown. Allow the bread to cool.

Slice and serve alongside a meal or as a snack. Store any leftover bread in an airtight container or wrapped in plastic wrap for up to 3 days.

Makes 8 to 10 servings

Dill and Onion Dinner Rolls

Sometimes there's nothing better than a warm dinner roll straight out of the oven, slathered with butter. Unfortunately, few dinner rolls follow a Paleo plan. Here is one of the exceptions. These savory rolls are the perfect companions to any hearty dish, but especially to a nice winter stew. You can substitute almost any herb you'd like for the dill—and use garlic powder instead of onion powder, if desired—for an interesting and delicious variation.

- 3 large eggs
- 1 tablespoon raw honey
- 1 tablespoon water
- 2 tablespoons unsalted butter, melted
- 2 cups blanched almond flour
- 1/4 cup coconut flour
- 1 cup ground golden flaxseed
- 1 tablespoon ground dill
- 1 teaspoon onion powder
- 1 teaspoon baking soda

Preheat the oven to 400 degrees F. Lightly grease a 9-inch round cake pan with cooking spray or coconut oil and set aside.

In a medium bowl, using an electric mixer, beat the eggs until light yellow and frothy. Add the honey, water, and melted butter, and stir to combine.

In a large bowl, stir together the almond and coconut flours, flaxseed, dill, onion powder, and baking soda until well combined.

Add the egg mixture to the dry ingredients and stir until well combined. Allow the dough to rest for 5 minutes, then stir again, adding a little more water if necessary to make the dough pliable and easy to knead. The dough should be lightly sticky but not wet. Allow the dough to rest for 5 more minutes.

Divide the dough into 12 equal pieces. Lightly knead each piece of dough into a ball, dusting with a little almond flour if necessary to keep the dough soft. Nestle the dough rolls into the prepared pan.

Bake for 20 to 25 minutes, or until the tops of the rolls are browned. Serve warm or at room temperature. Store any leftover rolls in an airtight container or wrapped in plastic wrap for up to 3 days.

Makes 1 dozen rolls

Herb Bread

This light and fragrant loaf is the perfect addition to a healthful meal and can be customized to complement whatever you're serving. It doesn't take as long to bake as traditional breads and it's Paleo friendly and gluten-free. Fresh herbs are best, though dried will do in a pinch. Feel free to add to or substitute the ones listed here for your favorites.

- 1/4 cup blanched almond flour
- 1/4 cup arrowroot flour
- 1 teaspoon baking soda
- 3/4 cup natural raw cashew butter
- 1 tablespoon raw honey
- 3 large eggs
- 2 tablespoons finely chopped thyme
- 1 tablespoon finely chopped oregano
- 1 tablespoon finely chopped rosemary
- 3 tablespoons olive oil

Preheat the oven to 350 degrees F. Line a 9 x 13–inch jelly roll pan with parchment paper and set aside.

In a small bowl, stir together the almond and arrowroot flours and baking soda until combined.

In a large bowl, using an electric mixer, beat the cashew butter and honey, then add the eggs, one at a time, mixing after each addition. Add the thyme, oregano, and rosemary, and stir until combined.

Add the flour mixture to the wet ingredients and stir until a wet dough forms.

Drizzle the olive oil on the parchment-lined pan and spread the dough over it. Bake for 25 to 30 minutes, or until the top of the bread is golden brown. Allow the bread to cool.

Slice and serve alongside a meal or as a snack. Store any leftover bread in an airtight container or wrapped in plastic wrap for up to 3 days.

Makes 12 servings

High-Fiber Breakfast Muffins

These muffins come together super fast and are perfect for a busy morning when you want something substantial but don't have time to prepare a large breakfast. Tart cranberries and crunchy pecans add flavor and substance to these high-fiber coconut-flour muffins made with flaxseed.

- 1/2 cup coconut flour
- 1/4 cup ground golden flaxseed
- 2 teaspoons baking powder
- 6 large eggs
- 1/2 cup coconut oil
- 1/2 cup chopped pecans, toasted if desired
- 1/2 cup dried cranberries

Preheat the oven to 350 degrees F. Lightly grease a muffin pan with cooking spray or coconut oil and set aside.

In a medium bowl, stir together the coconut flour, flaxseed, and baking powder until combined.

In a large bowl, using an electric mixer, beat the eggs and coconut oil. Add the flour mixture to the wet ingredients and stir until well combined. Gently fold in the pecans and cranberries.

Spoon the batter into the muffin tins, filling each cup about halfway. Bake for 12 to 15 minutes, or until the muffin tops are lightly browned.

Allow the muffins to cool for 10 minutes before removing from the pan. Store any leftover muffins in an airtight container or wrapped in plastic wrap for up to 3 days, or freeze in a resealable plastic bag for up to 3 months.

Makes 1 dozen muffins

Pecan Cinnamon Rolls

While these aren't the giant cinnamon buns you see at shopping malls, they are a deliciously sweet treat perfect for brunch or a Sunday morning when you want to indulge without overdoing it. Enjoy these warm from the oven, or reheat leftovers in the microwave for a few seconds.

Dough:
- 2 large eggs
- 1 tablespoon raw honey
- 1/4 cup coconut oil
- 2 cups blanched almond flour
- 1 teaspoon baking soda

Filling:
- 2 tablespoons coconut oil, melted
- 2 tablespoons ground cinnamon
- 3 tablespoons coconut sugar
- 1/2 cup pecans, coarsely chopped

Icing:
- 1/4 cup canned full-fat coconut milk
- 1/4 cup coconut sugar
- 1 tablespoon pure vanilla extract
- 1 teaspoon arrowroot flour

Preheat the oven to 350 degrees F. Line a baking sheet with parchment paper and set aside.

Dough

In a large bowl, using an electric mixer, beat the eggs and honey. Add the coconut oil and stir to combine.

In a medium bowl, stir together the almond flour and baking soda. Add the flour mixture to the wet ingredients, and stir until a stiff dough forms.

Lay a large piece of parchment paper on a clean surface and place the dough on it. Lay another piece of parchment on top, then roll out the dough until you have a rectangle about 1/4-inch thick.

Filling

Combine the coconut oil, cinnamon, and sugar, and sprinkle over the rolled-out dough. Sprinkle with the chopped pecans.

Roll up the dough, starting with the longer side of the rectangle, and slice into 8 to 10 (2-inch-thick) cinnamon rolls. Position the rolls on the prepared pan.

Bake for 15 to 20 minutes, or until the rolls are lightly browned.

Icing

Meanwhile, to make the icing, in a small bowl, stir together the coconut milk, sugar, vanilla, and arrowroot flour until well combined.

Using a spoon or spatula, drizzle the icing over the warm cinnamon rolls. Serve warm. Store any leftover rolls in an airtight container or wrapped in plastic wrap for up to 3 days.

Makes about 8 rolls

Buttermilk Biscuits

If you find yourself missing tender and buttery biscuits on the Paleo diet, have no fear. After eating one of these wonderful biscuits, you will rejoice that you've found such a suitable replacement. These are perfect for Sunday-morning breakfast or a healthful brunch when you want to impress.

- 6 egg whites
- 1/2 cup low-fat buttermilk
- 1 1/2 cups blanched almond flour
- 1/4 cup coconut flour
- 2 teaspoons baking powder
- 2 tablespoons chilled coconut oil or butter

Preheat the oven to 350 degrees F. Line a baking sheet with parchment paper and set aside.

In a medium bowl, using an electric mixer, beat the egg whites and buttermilk until well combined.

In a large bowl, stir together the almond and coconut flours and baking powder until combined. Add the cold coconut oil and mix with a fork until the mixture resembles coarse crumbs.

Add the egg mixture to the dry ingredients and stir until a wet dough forms.

Using an ice cream scoop, scoop rounded portions of the dough onto the prepared pan. Bake for 10 to 15 minutes, or until the tops of the biscuits are lightly browned. Allow the biscuits to cool for a few minutes before serving.

Serve warm with butter or Paleo-approved jam. Store any leftover biscuits in an airtight container or wrapped in plastic wrap for up to 3 days, or freeze in a resealable plastic bag for up to 3 months.

Makes 8 biscuits

Cinnamon Raisin Bread

This lightly sweetened Paleo-approved cinnamon raisin bread is ideal as morning toast or even using for French toast. You can substitute cranberries for the raisins if desired, or even add walnuts or pecans for crunch and flavor.

- 2 cups blanched almond flour
- 2 tablespoons coconut flour
- 1/4 cup ground golden flaxseed
- 1 tablespoon ground cinnamon
- 2 teaspoons baking soda
- 1/4 cup coconut oil, melted
- 1 tablespoon apple cider vinegar
- 5 large eggs
- 2 tablespoons raw honey
- 1 cup unsweetened raisins

Preheat the oven to 350 degrees F. Lightly grease a standard loaf pan with cooking spray or coconut oil and set aside.

In a large bowl, stir together the almond and coconut flours, flaxseed, cinnamon, and baking soda until well combined.

In a medium bowl, combine the melted coconut oil and apple cider vinegar. Add the eggs and beat until well combined. Stir in the honey.

Add the egg mixture to the dry ingredients and stir until well combined. Fold in the raisins.

Pour the batter into the prepared pan. Bake for 25 to 30 minutes, or until the top of the bread is well browned.

Allow the bread to cool for 10 minutes before removing it from the pan. Slice and serve warm with butter. Store any leftover slices in an airtight container or wrapped in plastic wrap for up to 3 days or freeze in a resealable plastic bag for up to 3 months.

Makes 1 loaf (8-10 slices)

Apple Cinnamon Bread

Applesauce makes for moist and delicious bread that is great for breakfast or as a snack, and the pure maple syrup adds a subtle sweetness that nicely complements the loaf. For best results, be sure to buy unsweetened applesauce, or better yet, make it yourself.

- 2 cups blanched almond flour
- 1 tablespoon ground cinnamon
- 1 teaspoon baking soda
- 2 large eggs
- 1/2 cup cold water
- 1/4 cup pure maple syrup
- 1 teaspoon pure vanilla extract
- 1/2 cup unsweetened applesauce
- 1 Granny Smith apple, peeled, cored, and chopped
- 1/4 cup chopped walnuts

Preheat the oven to 350 degrees F. Lightly grease a standard loaf pan with cooking spray or coconut oil and set aside.

In a medium bowl, sift together the almond flour, cinnamon, and baking soda until well combined.

In a large bowl, using an electric mixer, beat the eggs until frothy. Add the water, maple syrup, and vanilla, and stir until well combined. Stir in the applesauce, then fold in the chopped apple.

Carefully add the flour mixture to the wet ingredients and stir until just combined. Pour the batter into the prepared pan, sprinkle the walnuts over the top, and bake for 35 to 40 minutes, or until the top of the bread is browned and the edges are crisp. A toothpick inserted into the center should come out clean.

Allow the bread to cool completely on a wire rack before removing it from the pan. Slice and serve. Store any leftover slices in an airtight container or wrapped in plastic wrap for up to 3 days.

Makes 1 loaf (8-10 slices)

Classic Cream Scones

While these scones are made with coconut milk instead of heavy cream, it's unlikely that you'll be able to tell the difference. Moist and tender, these pair beautifully with your morning coffee or a late-afternoon tea. While this base recipe is for plain scones, it lends itself to numerous variations. Feel free to add half a cup or so of dried currants, raisins, or nuts, if desired.

- 6 egg whites
- 1/2 cup canned full-fat coconut milk
- 1 1/2 cups blanched almond flour
- 1/4 cup coconut flour
- 2 teaspoons baking powder
- 2 tablespoons chilled coconut oil

Preheat the oven to 350 degrees F. Line a baking sheet with parchment paper and set aside.

In a medium bowl, using an electric mixer, beat the egg whites and coconut milk until combined.

In a large bowl, stir together the almond and coconut flours and baking powder until combined. Add the cold coconut oil and mix with a fork until the mixture resembles coarse crumbs.

Add the egg mixture to the dry ingredients and stir until a wet dough forms.

Using an ice cream scoop, scoop rounded portions of the dough onto the prepared pan. Bake for 10 to 15 minutes, or until the tops of the scones are lightly browned. Allow the scones to cool for a few minutes before serving.

Serve warm with butter or Paleo-approved jam. Store any leftover scones in an airtight container or wrapped in plastic wrap for up to 3 days or freeze in a resealable plastic bag for up to 3 months.

Makes 8 scones

Maple Walnut Bread

Sweet maple syrup and crunchy walnuts come together in a bread that is delightfully moist without being too sweet. This bread is delicious toasted, served plain, or with butter or jam, or prepared as French toast. Add raisins or dried cranberries if you're looking for something a little bit different.

- 2 cups blanched almond flour
- 1 tablespoon ground cinnamon
- 1 teaspoon baking soda
- 2 large eggs
- 1/2 cup cold water
- 1 teaspoon pure vanilla extract
- 1/4 cup pure maple syrup
- 2 overripe bananas, mashed
- 1 cup chopped walnuts, divided

Preheat the oven to 350 degrees F. Lightly grease a standard loaf pan with cooking spray or coconut oil and set aside.

In a medium bowl, sift together the almond flour, cinnamon, and baking soda until well combined.

In a large bowl, using an electric mixer, beat the eggs until light yellow and frothy. Add the water, vanilla, and maple syrup, and beat until well combined. Stir in the mashed bananas, then fold in half a cup of the chopped walnuts.

Carefully add the flour mixture to the wet ingredients and stir until just combined. Pour the batter into the prepared pan, sprinkle with the remaining walnuts, and bake for 35 to 40 minutes, or until the top of the bread is browned and the edges are crisp. A toothpick inserted into the center of the bread should come out clean.

Allow the bread to cool completely on a wire rack before removing it from the pan. Slice and serve. Store any leftover slices in an airtight container or wrapped in plastic wrap for up to 3 days.

Makes 1 loaf (8 to 10 slices)

Basic Paleo Pizza Dough

Pizza is a favorite for many and one of the hardest things to give up on a Paleo diet. While many toppings are Paleo friendly, pizza crust is not—that is, until now. This basic dough will satisfy your pizza cravings and make you wonder why you ever relied on delivery. This recipe makes two decent-size crusts, and it freezes well, so you can save one for later.

- 3 large eggs
- 2 cups blanched almond flour
- 1/4 cup coconut flour
- 2 tablespoons unsalted butter, melted
- 1 tablespoon water

Preheat the oven to 400 degrees F.

In a medium bowl, using an electric mixer, beat the eggs until light yellow and frothy.

In a large bowl, stir together the almond and coconut flours and melted butter until well combined. Stir in the water.

Add the eggs to the flour mixture and stir until well combined. Allow the dough to rest for 5 minutes, then stir again, adding a little more water if necessary to make the dough pliable and easy to knead. The dough should be lightly sticky, but not wet. Allow the dough to rest for 5 more minutes.

Divide the dough into 2 equal pieces. Lightly knead each piece into a ball, dusting with a little almond flour if necessary to keep the dough soft. Roll out to desired thickness.

Top the dough as desired, place directly on a pizza stone or pizza pan, and bake until the crust edges are lightly browned and crisp. Store any leftover dough in an airtight container or a resealable plastic bag in the refrigerator for up to 2 days or in the freezer for up to 3 months.

Makes 2 large pizza crusts

Rustic Artisan Loaf

This bread is great for cutting into cubes and dipping in olive oil mixed with herbs and seasonings to set out when you're having company. The recipe calls for baking the dough free-form for a more authentic presentation, but you can also bake it in a standard loaf pan for easy slicing, if that's more your cup of tea.

- 3 large eggs
- 2 cups blanched almond flour
- 1/4 cup coconut flour
- 2 tablespoons unsalted butter, melted
- 1 tablespoon water
- 1 tablespoon raw honey

Preheat the oven to 400 degrees F. Position a pizza stone on the center oven rack, or line a baking sheet with parchment paper and set aside.

In a medium bowl, using an electric mixer, beat the eggs until light yellow and frothy.

In a large bowl, stir together the almond and coconut flours and melted butter until well combined. Stir in the water.

Add the eggs and honey to the flour mixture and stir until well combined. Allow the dough to rest for 5 minutes, then stir again, adding a little more water if necessary to make the dough pliable and easy to knead. The dough should be lightly sticky, but not wet. Allow the dough to rest for 5 more minutes.

Divide the dough into 2 equal pieces. Lightly knead each one into a ball, dusting with a little almond flour if necessary to keep the dough soft.

Place the loaves directly on the pizza stone or prepared pan, and slash the tops with a sharp paring knife. Bake the loaves for 25 to 30 minutes, until very browned and slightly hollow sounding when tapped on the bottom.

Allow the bread to cool completely. In order to preserve freshness, slice only what is being served. Store any leftover bread in a resealable plastic bag or wrapped in plastic wrap for up to 3 days.

Makes 2 medium loaves

Classic Dinner Rolls

Pureed pumpkin adds subtle sweetness and moisture to these dinner rolls, which are perfect for a holiday meal, special celebration, or just a regular weeknight.

- 3 large eggs
- 1/2 cup pumpkin puree (canned or freshly roasted)
- 2 cups blanched almond flour
- 1/4 cup coconut flour
- 2 tablespoons unsalted butter, melted
- 1 tablespoon water

Preheat the oven to 400 degrees F. Lightly grease a 9-inch round cake pan with cooking spray or coconut oil and set aside.

In a medium bowl, using an electric mixer, beat the eggs until light yellow and frothy. Add the pumpkin puree and stir until well combined.

In a large bowl, stir together the almond and coconut flours and melted butter until well combined. Stir in the water.

Add the egg mixture to the flour mixture and stir until well combined. Allow the dough to rest for 5 minutes, then stir again, adding a little more water if necessary to make the dough pliable and easy to knead. The dough should be lightly sticky, but not wet. Allow the dough to rest for 5 more minutes.

Divide the dough into 12 equal pieces. Lightly knead each piece of dough into a ball, dusting with a little almond flour if necessary to keep the dough soft. Nestle the dough rolls into the prepared pan.

Bake for 20 to 25 minutes, or until the tops of the rolls are browned. Cool completely before serving. Store any leftover rolls in an airtight container or wrapped in plastic wrap for up to 3 days.

Makes 1 dozen rolls

Country White Bread

While there are many types of breads that make great sandwiches, sometimes nothing beats a basic white country bread, which is exactly what this recipe is for. There are no special flavorings or fancy ingredients, but this bread is Paleo-approved and will make a delicious sandwich of almost anything. Of course, this bread goes beyond just sandwiches: use it for toast, stuffing, breadcrumbs, and more. The only difference is that you can feel good about eating this bread as opposed to the standard grocery store loaf.

- 1 cup blanched almond flour
- 1/2 cup arrowroot flour
- 1 teaspoon baking soda
- 1 teaspoon cream of tartar
- 3 large eggs
- 2 tablespoons safflower oil
- 2 tablespoons water
- 1 teaspoon raw honey

Preheat the oven to 350 degrees F. Lightly grease a standard loaf pan with cooking spray or coconut oil and set aside.

In a medium bowl, stir together the almond and arrowroot flours, baking soda, and cream of tartar until well combined.

In a large bowl, using an electric mixer, beat the eggs until frothy. Add the safflower oil, water, and honey, and stir to combine.

Add the flour mixture to the wet ingredients and stir until just combined. Pour the batter into the prepared pan and bake for 25 to 30 minutes, or until the top of the bread is golden brown.

Allow the bread to cool completely on a wire rack before removing it from the pan. In order to preserve freshness, slice only what is being served. Store any leftover bread in a resealable plastic bag or wrapped in plastic wrap for up to 3 days.

Makes 1 loaf (8-10 slices)

Paleo "Rye"

Rye bread is something many following the Paleo plan have resigned themselves to going without, which is a shame, because the flavor goes so well with many Paleo meals. This bread is not a true rye bread, as it is not made with rye flour, but it does mimic the flavor, thanks to the addition of caraway seeds. This makes terrific sandwich bread, but it's also great with a simple pat of softened butter.

- 1 cup blanched almond flour
- 1/2 cup ground golden flaxseed
- 1 teaspoon baking soda
- 1 teaspoon cream of tartar
- 3 large eggs

- 2 tablespoons olive oil
- 2 tablespoons water
- 1 teaspoon blackstrap molasses
- 1 tablespoon caraway seeds

Preheat the oven to 350 degrees F. Lightly grease a standard loaf pan with cooking spray or coconut oil and set aside.

In a medium bowl, stir together the flour, flaxseed, baking soda, and cream of tartar until well combined.

In a large bowl, using an electric mixer, beat the eggs until frothy. Add the olive oil, water, and molasses, and stir to combine.

Add the flour mixture to the wet ingredients and stir until well combined. Fold in the caraway seeds.

Pour the batter into the prepared pan and bake for 25 to 30 minutes, or until the top of the bread is dark brown.

Allow the bread to cool completely on a wire rack before removing it from the pan. In order to preserve freshness, slice only what is being served. Store any leftover bread in a resealable plastic bag or wrapped in plastic wrap for up to 3 days.

Makes 1 loaf (8 to 10 slices)

Kalamata Olive Sandwich Bread

This savory bread is best for sandwiches featuring high-quality Italian meats or just as a snack when you crave something with a lot of flavor. Feel free to substitute different types of olives in this recipe, or even use a combination for more flavor and variation. You can also bake this bread in a jelly roll pan for a more focaccia-like loaf that is great for serving alongside hearty soups and stews.

- 1/4 cup blanched almond flour
- 1/4 cup arrowroot flour
- 1 teaspoon baking soda
- 3 large eggs

- 3/4 cup natural raw cashew butter
- 1/2 cup pitted and chopped kalamata olives
- 3 tablespoons olive oil

Preheat the oven to 350 degrees F. Lightly grease a standard loaf pan with olive oil or cooking spray and set aside.

In a medium bowl, stir together the almond and arrowroot flours and baking soda until well combined.

In a large bowl, using an electric mixer, beat the eggs and cashew butter until well combined.

Add the flour mixture to the wet ingredients and stir until a wet dough forms. Fold in the olives.

Spread the batter into the prepared pan and drizzle the olive oil over the top. Bake for 25 to 30 minutes, or until the top of the bread is golden brown.

Allow the bread to cool completely on a wire rack before removing it from the pan. Slice and serve. Store any leftover slices in an airtight container or wrapped in plastic wrap for up to 3 days.

Makes 1 loaf (8-10 slices)

Quinoa Sandwich Bread

Quinoa is a superfood in its own right. It's high in protein and fiber, and it doesn't contain the same starchiness as rice or other grains since it's actually a seed. This makes it ideal for Paleo dieters. This bread is made with finely ground quinoa "flour," which makes a beautiful, healthful loaf that is suited for any meal.

- 1 cup whole white quinoa
- 2 large eggs
- 1/4 cup coconut flour
- 1 tablespoon unsalted butter, melted
- 1 tablespoon water
- 1 tablespoon raw honey

Preheat the oven to 350 degrees F. Lightly grease a standard loaf pan with cooking spray or coconut oil and set aside.

Place the quinoa in a powerful blender, food processor, or clean coffee grinder, and process until it becomes a fine flour. Alternately, substitute pre-ground quinoa flour.

In a medium bowl, using an electric mixer, beat the eggs until light yellow and frothy.

In a large bowl, stir together the quinoa and coconut flours and melted butter until well combined. Stir in the water.

Add the eggs and honey to the flour mixture and stir until well combined. Allow the dough to rest for 5 minutes, then stir again, adding a little more water if necessary to make the dough pliable and easy to knead. The dough should be lightly sticky, but not wet. Allow the dough to rest for 5 more minutes.

Place the dough in the prepared pan and bake for 30 to 35 minutes, or until the top of the bread is golden brown.

Allow the bread to cool completely on a wire rack before removing it from the pan. In order to preserve freshness, slice only what is being served. Store any leftover bread in an airtight container or wrapped in plastic wrap for up to 3 days.

Makes 1 loaf (8-10 slices)

Honey "Wheat" Sandwich Bread

While we know the dangers of wheat in our diets, sometimes a sandwich calls for a nice soft honey wheat bread in order to fit the bill and satisfy a craving. While this is not a true wheat bread, the flaxseed adds the same kind of bulk and fiber that wheat does, but without the gluten. Flaxseed provides some heart-healthful fats as well. Though this isn't quite like the wheat bread you may be used to, we think you'll agree that it makes an excellent substitute.

- 1 cup blanched almond flour
- 1/2 cup ground golden flaxseed
- 1 teaspoon baking soda
- 1 teaspoon cream of tartar
- 3 large eggs
- 2 tablespoons safflower oil
- 2 tablespoons water
- 2 tablespoons raw honey

Preheat the oven to 350 degrees F. Lightly grease a standard loaf pan with cooking spray or coconut oil and set aside.

In a medium bowl, stir together the flour, flaxseed, baking soda, and cream of tartar until well combined.

In a large bowl, using an electric mixer, beat the eggs until frothy. Add the safflower oil, water, and honey, and stir until well combined.

Add the flour mixture to the wet ingredients and stir until well combined. Pour the batter into the prepared pan and bake for 25 to 30 minutes, or until the top of the bread is dark brown.

Allow the bread to cool completely on a wire rack before removing it from the pan. In order to preserve freshness, slice only what is being served. Store any leftover bread in a resealable plastic bag or wrapped in plastic wrap for up to 3 days.

Makes 1 loaf (8 to 10 slices)

CONCLUSION

Transitioning from a standard Western diet to a healthful but seemingly drastic way of life such as the Paleo diet can be difficult, but if you have the willpower to do it, the results will be incredible. Really, all you need is to want to be healthy more than you want to eat that cupcake.

Diseases of excess, such as obesity, gastric disorders, and type 2 diabetes, are raging out of control. The Paleo diet originated because a gastroenterologist was looking for a better way to treat his patients, but it really took off in the late 1980s and early 1990s when people began looking for a healthier way to live.

Fortunately, we're learning more about how our bodies work every day and are slowly unraveling the mysteries behind such diseases as depression, celiac, and even muscular dystrophy. The findings are surprising. Research indicates that what we eat plays a huge role in how we feel, and the more we research, the stronger those connections become.

One of the main reasons that people struggle with transitioning to the Paleo diet is that they don't want to give up bread, but now that's simply not necessary. Breads made from almond and coconut flours can taste just as delicious as breads made from traditional white flour and refined sugar, but they don't have the disastrously unhealthful side effects.

Going Paleo is a perfect opportunity to avoid many diseases before they even set in, and since that the idea has gone mainstream, caveman-friendly products abound. So now that you know that you don't have to face the prospect of a life without sandwiches, what are you waiting for? All that you have to lose is weight and sickness!

CPSIA information can be obtained at www.ICGtesting.com
Printed in the USA
BVOW041043130213

313161BV00001B/94/P